INTERMEDIATE

A Quiet Christmas

— Carol Reflections for Solo Piano —

Lloyd Larson

Editor: Lloyd Larson
Music Engraving: MacMusic, Inc.
Cover Design: Ashley Donahue

ISBN: 978-0-7877-6321-3

lillenas
PUBLISHING COMPANY
www.lorenz.com

Foreword

I love the festive nature of Christmas: the energy, the fast pace, the joy, the numerous activities.... all of it! It is exhilarating and in so many ways enhances the celebration of Christ's birth. But, as in all of life, there is a flip side to that coin. And that is the serenity of Christmas: finding that island of peace and quiet in the ocean of activity as we reflect on the significance of the incarnation story: God becoming human and living among us.

As a practicing church musician my entire adult life, I have found Advent to be a sprint right up to Christmas Day. Typically there have been rehearsals, concerts, rehearsals, special worship services, rehearsals, family gatherings, and more rehearsals! In the midst of all of that, I have found it critical to find those quiet moments when I could personally embrace the significance of Christmas even as I moved from one commitment to the next.

I've had a habit for years following the final Christmas Eve worship service to come home and find as many of the collegiate Christmas programs as I could on TV and watch them as I decompressed from the activities of the season. And, because I tend to be an early riser, on Christmas morning I have typically retrieved the many cards and letters that have arrived over the recent weeks to read again the messages delivered from family and friends near and afar. It has become a meaningful part of my personal journey to the manger of the newborn Christ-child.

The importance of these solemn moments for me at Christmas has been the catalyst for this particular project, ***A Quiet Christmas***. Like Mary, following the energized visit by the shepherds as they shared their dramatic encounter with the angels, it is important that we find quiet moments to treasure and ponder the mystery of the Christmas story: *Unto you is born this day in the city of David a Savior, who is Christ the Lord.*

– Lloyd Larson

About the Arranger

Lloyd Larson is a freelance composer/arranger and the Keyboard Editor for Lillenas Publishing Company. His publications include well over 1,500 choral octavos, Christmas and Easter cantatas, numerous keyboard collections, several vocal solo and duet collections, instrumental solo and ensemble publications, orchestrations, and handbell settings. It is his work in the local church, though, that continues to be the catalyst for much of his writing. He is an active participant in his own home church where he directs the adult choir in addition to regularly being involved in worship planning and leadership. Lloyd has a B.A. from Anderson University (Indiana) and an M.C.M. from Southern Baptist Theological Seminary in Louisville, Kentucky.

Lloyd and his wife, Marci, live in the Minneapolis, Minnesota area. They have three children and five grandchildren.

Contents

Silent Night! Holy Night!

with

Still, Still, Still

FRANZ GRUBER
Arr. by Lloyd Larson

Serenely, freely ♩ = ca.69

18
cresc.
mp
22
poco rit.
mp
27
8va
a tempo
simile
mp
30
33
cresc.
mf

36
3
39
3
3
3
43
3
3
3
47
f
poco rit.
51
mf
a tempo
mp

*Music: Traditional Austrian Melody

Coventry Carol

Traditional English Melody
Arr. by Lloyd Larson

Expressively ♩ = ca. 88

17
21
25
mp
29
34

38
42
45
mf
47
49

52
54
56
58
cresc.
61
f

65
mf
69
73
dim. e rit.
mp
77
a tempo
81
rit. poco a poco al fine
p

The First Noel

W. SANDYS' *Christmas Carols*, 1833
Arr. by Lloyd Larson

Gently, steadily ♩ = ca. 104

13
16
19
22
mf
25

28
poco rit.
mp
a tempo
32
35
mf
39
43

47
51
f
54
57
Slightly broader ♩ = ca. 96
60
cresc. poco a poco
rit.
ff

64
3
67
71
f
dim. e rit.
75
Tempo I ♩ = ca. 104
mp
78
molto rit.
p

See, Amid the Winter's Snow

with

O Come, Let Us Adore Him

JOHN GOSS
Arr. by Lloyd Larson

Tenderly, expressively ♩ = ca. 80

14
3
mf
17
mp
20
23
27
mel.

30
mel.
33
mf
36
39
mp
43
cresc. poco a poco

46
Broadly ♩ = ca. 76
3
rit.
f
49
52
cresc.
55
ff
59
dim. e rit.
a tempo

*Music attr. to JOHN F. WADE

It Came upon the Midnight Clear

RICHARD S. WILLIS
Arr. by Lloyd Larson

Pensively ♩ = ca. 84

17
21
mp
25
cresc.
rit.
29
sub.p a tempo
33
poco rit.
cresc.

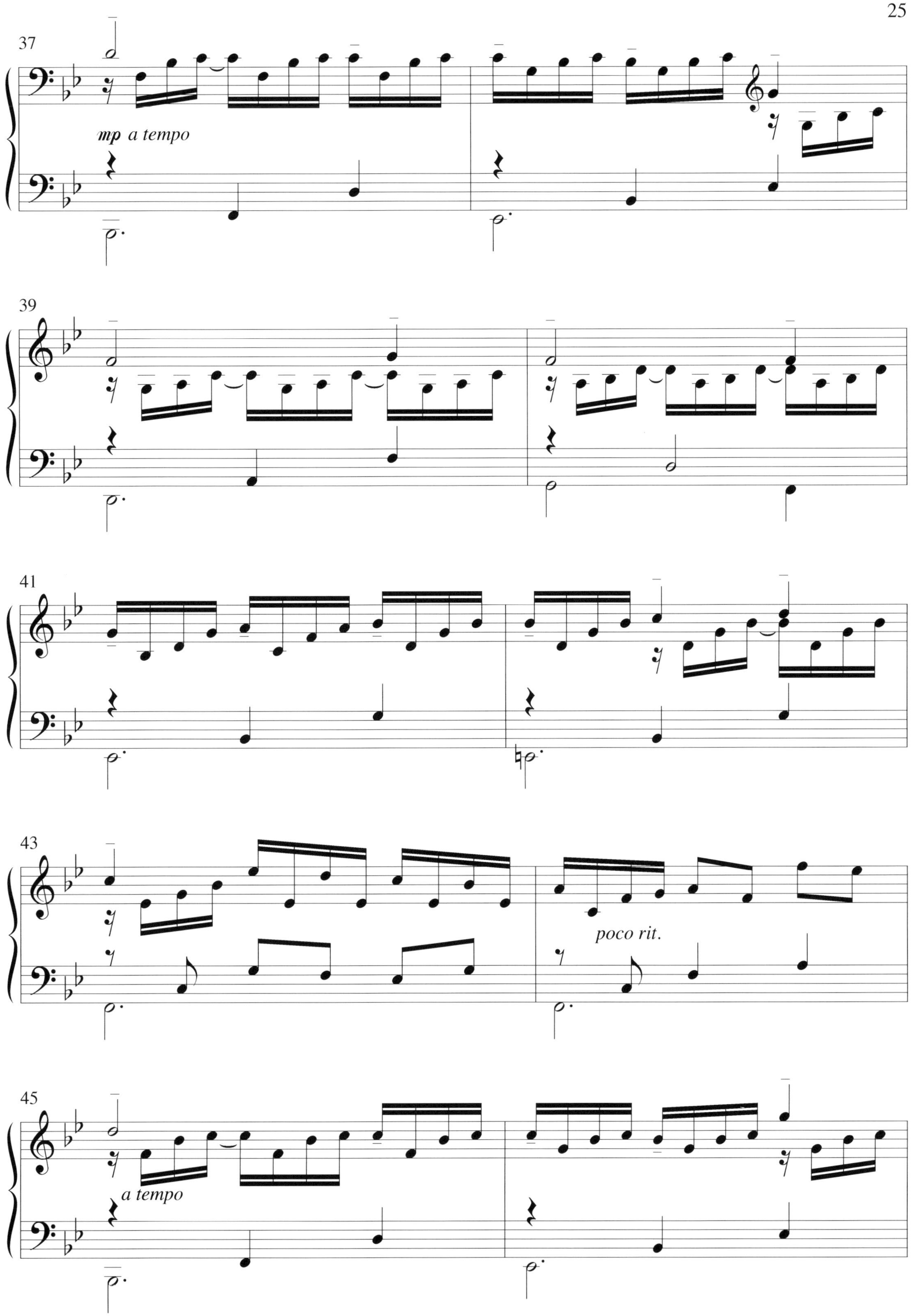
37
mp a tempo
39
41
43
poco rit.
45
a tempo

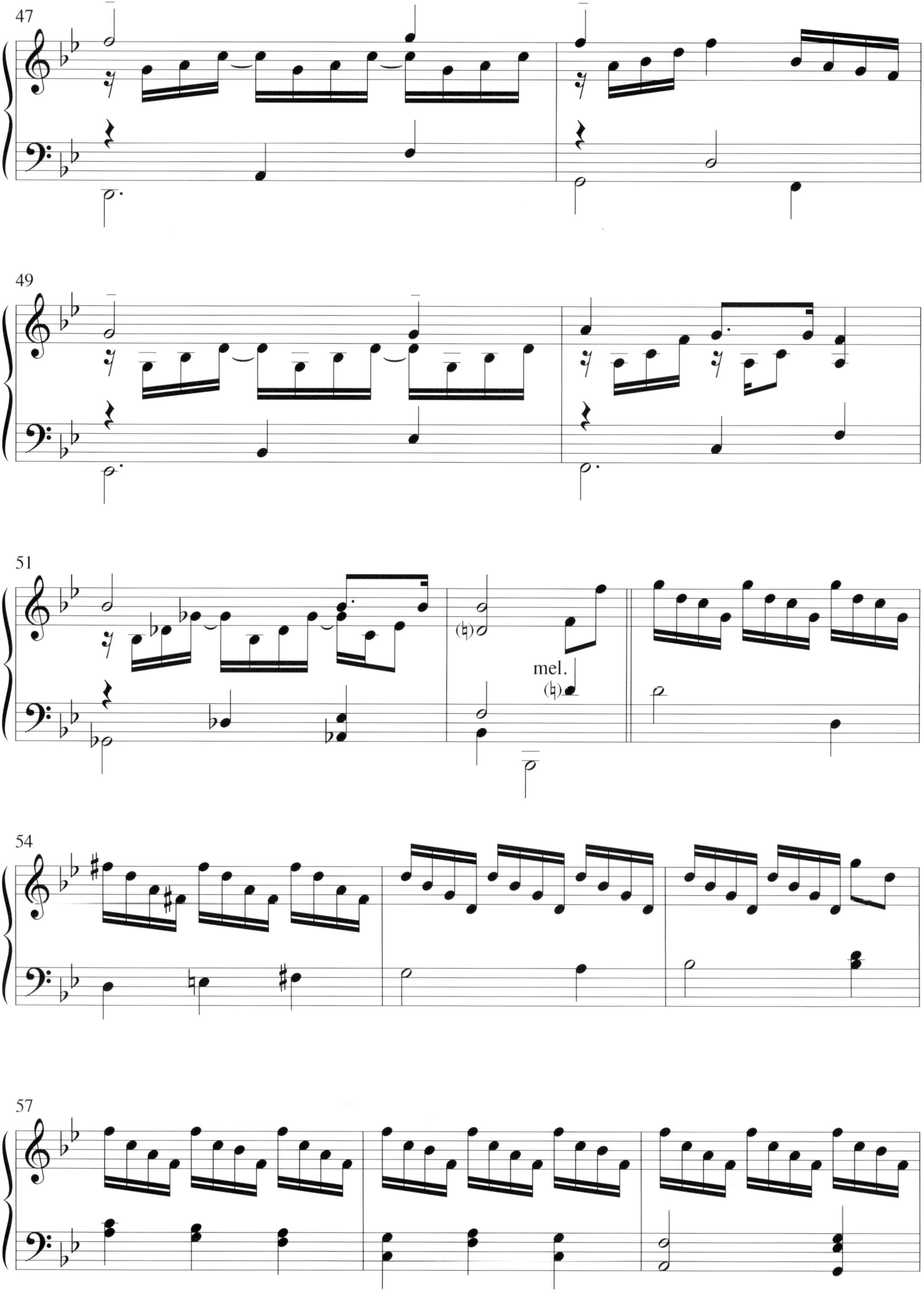
47
49
51
mel.
(♮)
(♮)
54
57

60
mel.
poco rit.
a tempo
mf
63
65
67
cresc. poco a poco
70
rit.
a tempo
f

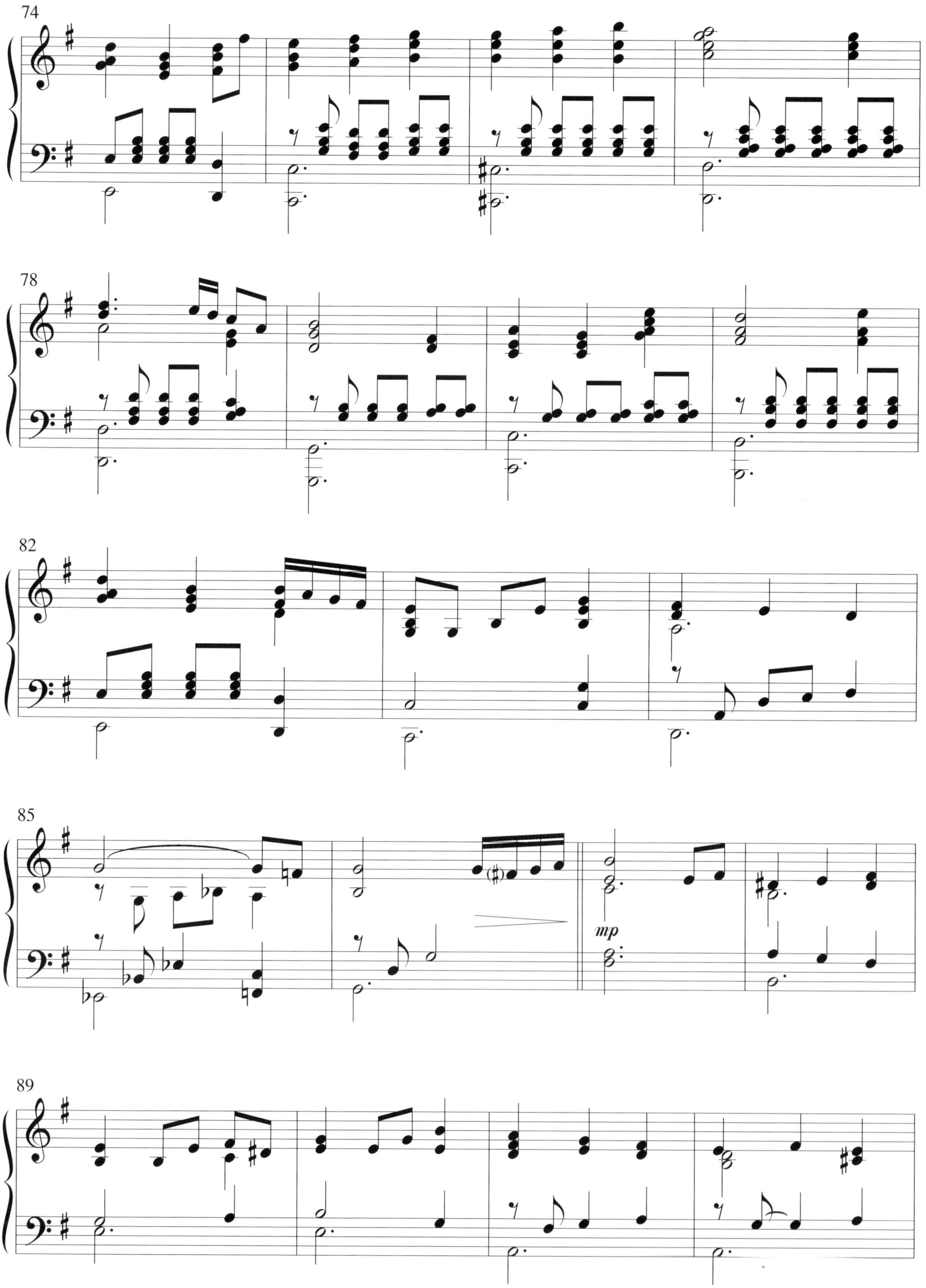
74
78
82
85
mp
89

93
(♮)
cresc.
rit.
sub. p a tempo
97
101
cresc. poco a poco
mp rit.
105
p a tempo
109
molto rit.
pp

Joy to the World

GEORGE FREDERICK HANDEL
Arr. by Lloyd Larson

Tenderly, very freely ♩ = ca. 80

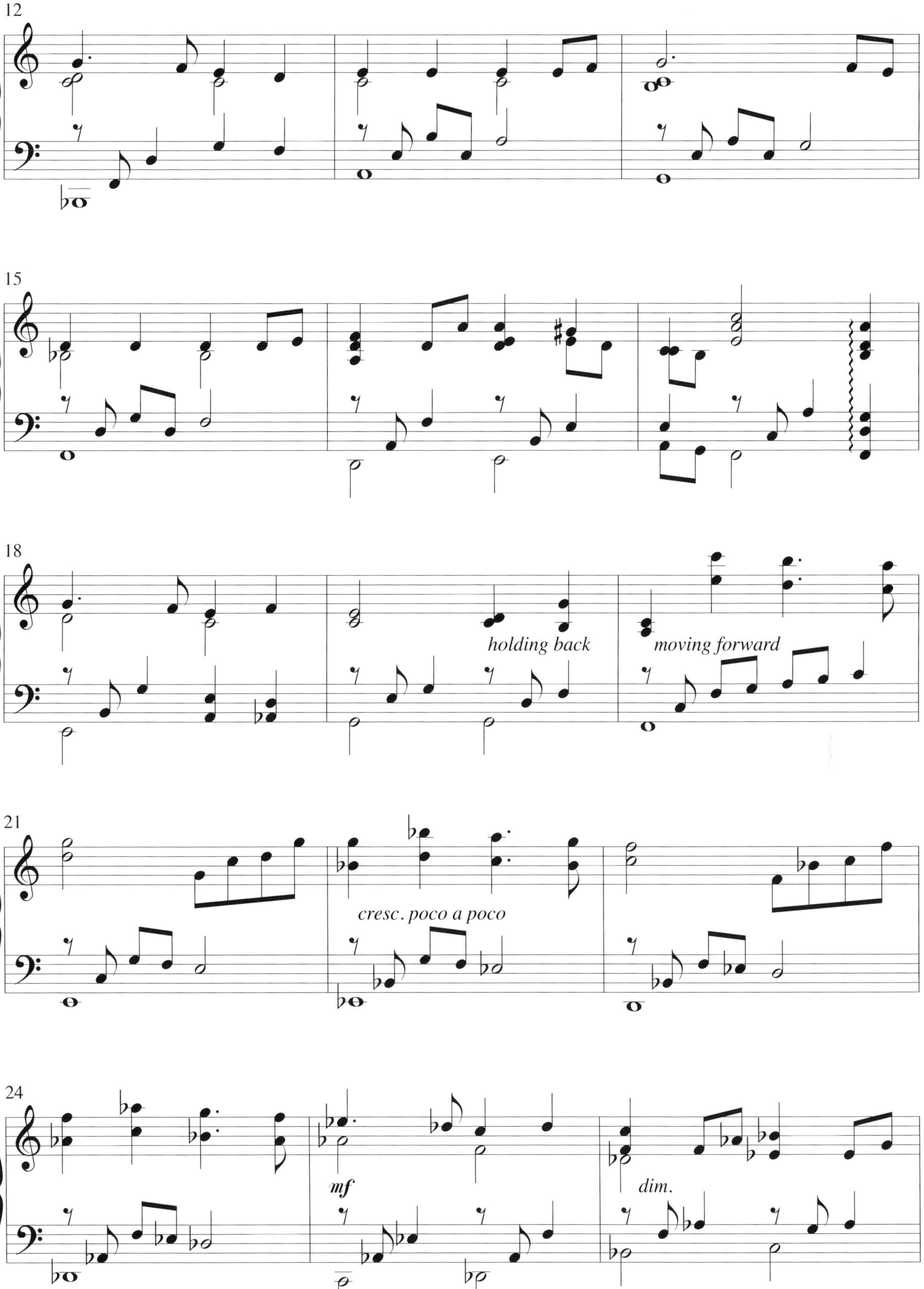
12
15
18
holding back
moving forward
21
cresc. poco a poco
24
mf
dim.

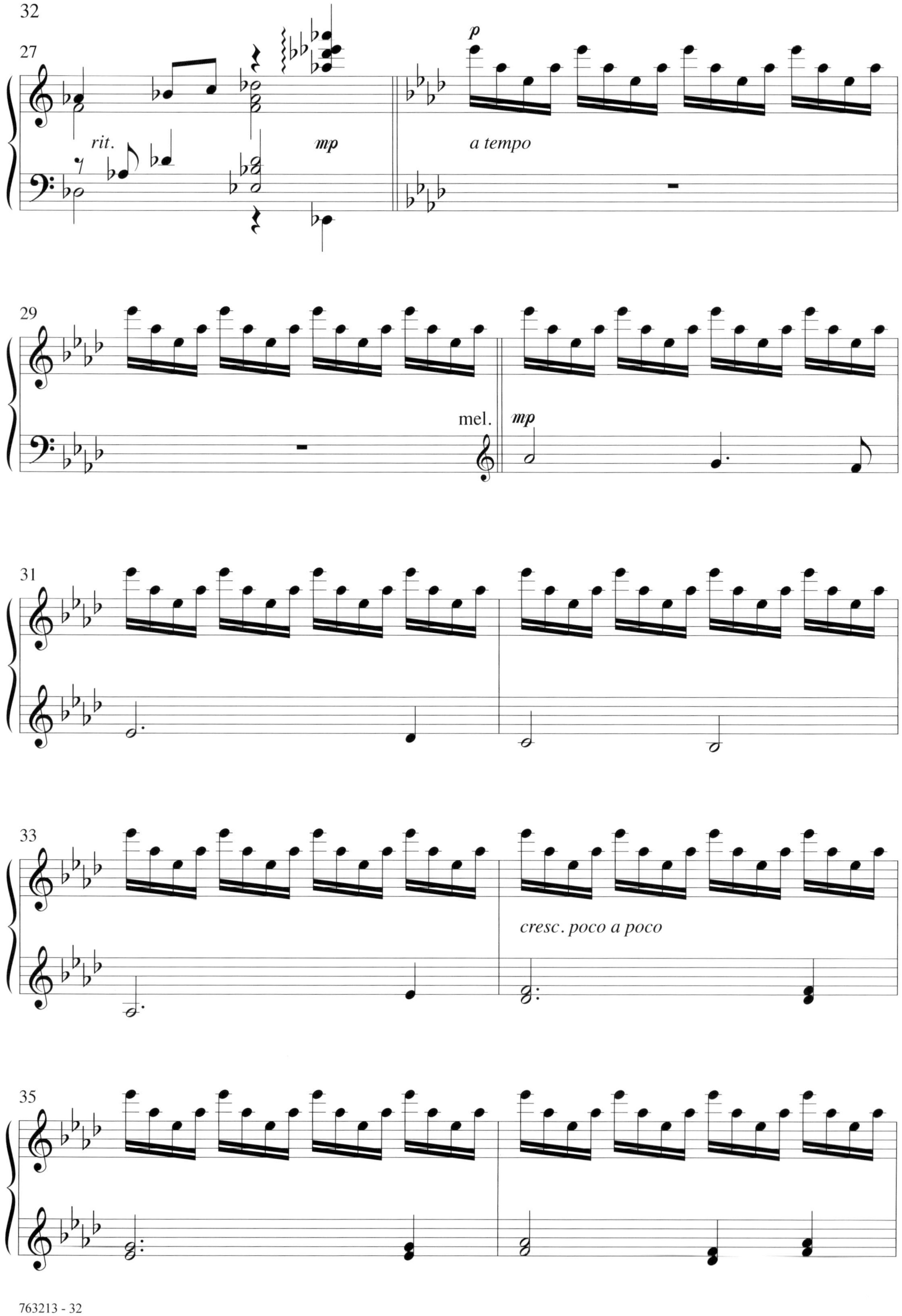
27
rit.
mp
p
a tempo
29
mel.
mp
31
33
cresc. poco a poco
35

37
mel.
mf
39
42
45
48
dim.
holding back
mp
moving forward

51
3
cresc. e rit.
3
mf a tempo
54
57
(♭)
cresc.
60
holding back
f moving forward
63
mf
mp

66
3
cresc.
69
mf
dim.
72
holding back
mp
moving forward
75
holding back
78
p
molto rit.

Wexford Carol

Traditional Irish Melody
Arr. by Lloyd Larson

Tenderly, with some freedom ♩ = ca. 63

17
21
mf
24
27
mel.
mp
mf
30
3

mel.
mf
f

44
46
3
49
51
Slowly, freely
8va
rit.
mp
54
(8va)
rit.
dim.
p

What Child Is This?

Traditional English Melody
Arr. by Lloyd Larson

With gentle, steady motion ♩ = ca. 112

17
21
mp
25
29
8va
p
mp
33

37
41
45
mf
49
53

57
dim. e rit.
61
mp a tempo
65
mf
69
73

76
79
82
cresc.
f
86
90

94
97
dim. poco a poco
rit.
101
a tempo
mp
105
dim. e rit.
p

In the Bleak Midwinter

GUSTAV T. HOLST
Arr. by Lloyd Larson

Pensively, very freely ♩ = ca. 80

16
Quickly, steadily ♩ = ca. 104
8va
20
mp
23
26
mp
mf
mel.
29
poco rit.

32
mel.
mp a tempo
35
cresc.
rit.
Slower ♩ = ca. 92
mf
38
molto rit.
Broadly ♩ = ca. 84
41
f
44

mp
mf
dim. poco a poco rit.
Slowly, freely
8va
p
pp

Lo! How a Rose E'er Blooming

Traditional German Carol, 15th c.
Arr. by Lloyd Larson

Tenderly, freely 𝅗𝅥 = ca. 52

13
16
19
22
mf
mel.
25
mel.

28
rit.
a tempo
31
f
34
mf
37
rit.
a tempo
40

42
mp
mf
mel.
44
46
mel.
mf
49

51
54
dim. e rit.
56
mp a tempo
58
L.H.
dim. poco a poco
60
p molto rit.
pp